www.tredition.de

AF185735

LAST APPEAL TO MANKIND

www.tredition.de

Author: © 2019 Diana M.
Publishing and printing: tredition GmbH,
Halenreie 40-44, 22359 Hamburg
The first English-language edition
Illustrations and Picture in book © Eternalia
Cover picture: Fotobanka Fotky Foto, Fotolia LLC

info@menschensohn.net
www.menschensohn.net

ISBN
978-3-7482-8733-9 Paperback
978-3-7482-8734-6 e-Book

LAST APPEAL

for the salvation of those who so far only recognized the teach-ings of the church, who completely forgot their task on earth and used everything received for this purpose only for their own goals, and all those who have not yet found the TRUTH.

IMANUEL:

"All over the earth, thousands will rise and announce me."

1st Part

ERRORS AND LIES

1. The Family of God, IMANUEL

To this day, all of us lie and confuse ourselves regarding the facts about earthly and supernatural affairs. Consider the existence of the Highest, God the Father and the whole family of God. Who belongs to the family of God? God the Father; His Son JESUS (the Love of God); the other Son of God, the Holy Spirit, IMANUEL (the Will of God); and the divine wife of God the Father, the Primordial Queen Elisabeth, the Divine mother.

IMANUEL, the Holy Spirit, had been married to Swanhild for twenty years, and they had the child IMANUEL. What do you think about crossing off two members of God's family from the family tree: IMANUEL and the Primordial Queen Elisabeth? It indicates great self-confidence, doesn't it? Who of you believes that, because of the lies of the church, individuals, and teachers, he will not suffer the aftermath himself? Of course, all those who fell for it. But he who sought and found the Truth has no reason to bear the after-effects of these lies.

To increase our confusion—to be more convincing and to keep their sponsors—the churches ascribed all the names of IMANUEL to Saint JESUS. And again, we fell for the lies.

IMANUEL is not JESUS! *IMANUEL is the Holy Spirit, the Spirit of Truth, Alpha and Omega, Parsifal, the Son of Man and Abdrushin.* It was very easy, then, for the churches to confuse us even more and to convince us of the second coming of Saint JESUS. Please note that *neither the book **In the Light of Truth - The Grail Message (1931)**, nor the book **Eternal Laws (1998)** explain it in this way. There, you will find the proof that Saint JESUS and IMANUEL are two different persons. After all, Saint JESUS only ever mentioned the Spirit of Truth in the third person. In the Gospel of John, chapter 16, verse 13, it is written: *"But when the Spirit of truth shall come, he shall guide you into all truth."* In the same chapter, verse 14, Saint JESUS says: *"He will glorify me (JESUS); for from mine (his teaching) he will take it and preach it to you."*

Yes. IMANUEL has been concealed from us for 2000 years. I personally think that they hide Him from the world because He is the Truth of God and Justice. He is the one who defeats the Darkness, binds Lucifer, and founds the Millennium Kingdom on earth—already foretold by the prophets—whereby He becomes King of this Kingdom.

Let us remember how many lies and distortions have already been uncovered, not only in the churches, but also in all other areas of life. The truth as energy is trying to break out into the earth, and justice comes with it. I have been on earth long enough, but I have never heard of the accumulation of so many natural disasters, wars, murders, suicides and unknown deadly diseases all at once.

IF THIS IS NOT THE WRATH AND JUSTICE OF THE LORD, THEN WHAT DOES THIS MEAN?

2. The Real Saviour of the Earth

The return of Saint Jesus, the Love of God, and the Fatima's Third Prophecy are closely connected. Why is that? Through the deliberate and great lie of many churches to mankind, for the purpose of appeasement. Many churches claim that Saint Jesus, the Love of God, comes as saviour—as if love could still help this earth. However, the Fatima's Third Prophecy predicts that Imanuel will cleanse the earth from Darkness, because He is the Will of God, his Truth and Justice. In the same event, both Sons of God are expected as saviours (*Eternal Laws, Volume 3*).

It must be clear to everyone that one of the allegations is a lie. After the churches also ascribed all the names of Imanuel to Saint Jesus, it was child's play to mislead humanity to keep it quiet and leave mankind unable to understand. And mankind believed the Church again. Thus, the churches achieved their goal, which was to keep humanity in darkness and ignorance. Does this show the spiritual indolence and superficiality of humanity? Of course—otherwise, humanity would not let it happen, and the Church would not be able to merge the both of the Sons of God so easily. It makes sense that only Imanuel can come to earth as Truth and Justice, and this, in turn, means that He is the true Saviour of the earth—but not for all of us!

Let us take the former chosen ones as an example. They either chose the Church's teachings as their only truth or, in the course of several earthly lives, they became materialists and atheists who were no longer interested in the spiritual at all. Thus, they not only failed to fulfil their duties but became enemies of both of the Sons of God, and Swanhild. Saint Jesus was murdered by mankind. Hardly anyone believed Imanuel and Swanhild during their lifetimes. God the Father thus erased the position of the chosen ones and degraded the 144,000 to simple spirits.

ANYONE WHO BASES THEIR BELIEFS AND CONVICTIONS ON LIES WILL BE VERY UNPLEASANTLY SURPRISED IN NO TIME AT ALL.

3. The most important difference between Elisabeth and Mary

If you think the Vatican doesn't know the truth, you're wrong. The Church continued to spread lies that were thought up and practiced (during the Inquisition) by the Jesuits in the Middle Ages.

Hopefully someone will read these texts to learn the truth. God the Father rejoices for each one of us who returns to Him through the Truth.

Therefore the most important difference between Elisabeth and Mary is their respective origin in Creation. *(see fig. Structure of the Creation)*

Elisabeth is the wife of God the Father. She was created by Him as the very first creature with female polarity of the energies. Since He wanted to create more beings, He needed the female (negative) energy, and this is the Primordial Queen Elisabeth.

Mary, the earthly mother of Jesus, **became Joseph's wife** so that he could protect her and, of course, the little child, because she was already in her third month of pregnancy with Saint Jesus. Three months before Mary's marriage to Joseph, she had found her truest, greatest love in the Roman Captain Creolus. For both of them, it was love at first sight. The Roman soldiers left Mary's village and the two never met again in their lives, although Creolus looked for Mary twice in her village at home. The second time, he learned that Mary was already married and pregnant.

Creolus was the biological father of Saint Jesus. You will find all the evidence and documents in the secret archive of the Vatican, some of which was opened to the public a few years ago.

IT SEEMS THAT THE MAJORITY OF PEOPLE (CHURCH BE- LIEVERS) WANT TO BELIEVE LIES. THAT MEANS: BELIEVE THE PRIESTS RATHER THAN THE TRUTH.

4. The Conception of Mary

At the beginning I would like to ask you a simple and logical question. Take Peter and Paul, for example: if Peter impregnates his wife, how can Paul become the father of the child? I'm sure you already know what I'm saying.

Almost all over the world, there is a legend that Mary, a virgin, became pregnant by the Holy Spirit. But the Sons of God, living in earthly bodies, also had to have biological parents who were humans living in earthly bodies. **This is required according to the Law of Attraction of Homogeneous Species**.

- The first time Imanuel incarnated as Abdrushin in Arabia was 3000 years ago. The Arabic name Abdrushin means "Son of Light". His earthly parents were Princess Dijanitra and Prince Ara-Masdah.
- Two thousand years ago, Saint Jesus incarnated on earth. His **earthly** parents were – Mary of Nazareth and Creolus.
- The second time Imanuel incarnated on earth as the *Spirit of Truth* was in 1875. His **earthly** parents were Therese and Theodor Bernhardt. Imanuel was given the earthly name *Oskar Ernst Bernhardt.*

Since the Middle Ages, the falsified legend about Mary has been around. And where were Princess Dijanitra and Therese Bernhardt? Also denied because of Imanuel?

AN INSOLENCE! TO THINK THAT LOGICALLY THINKING PEOPLE ARE SO STUPID.

5. What exactly does the word "projection" mean?

In the book *Eternal Laws, Volumes 1-3*, I read the word "projection" only in connection with false apparitions. Furthermore, the book also mentions that the preparation for the true earthly incarnation of the Sons of God takes thousands of earthly years.

It must become clear to everyone that apparitions of the true Saint Jesus or his earthly mother Mary in Amazonia (Indians) or in many places in Europe and America are impossible. The worst thing about it is the fact that only the Church, usually the Roman Catholic Church, decides on the authenticity of the apparitions.

While I was in a coma, three spiritual teachers stayed near me alternately. They told me they were the oldest ones (the wise) of Imanuel's team for the salvation of mankind. After my time in a coma, I received from the Lord, as a gift, abilities that are not usual on earth. They are called extra-sensory or supernatural abilities. But I only got these so that I could help many people who are still looking for the true way to the Lord.

While in my coma I asked my teacher how we could see which apparition was real and which was wrong. I also asked whether there were any spiritual apparitions. With great laughter I got the answer that there are only spiritual apparitions if the person is not incarnated. The only difference is in where the projection comes from (Light or Darkness). One such type of projection is, for example, the earthly fata morgana. It is, like all the others, ethereally. But the true apparitions, like those of the Primordial Queen Elisabeth in Fatima, bring very important messages to humanity, such as the coming of Imanuel as Saviour of the earth, and of the people who, in all their lives, served the Lord with devotion. The rest (indifferent and dark spirits) must sink back to the low planets from where they incarnated on earth, and where they themselves belong according to the Law of Gravity.

The Eternal Laws created by God cannot be learned at all in the churches. I wonder why. It is always about the same thing: striving for the greatest possible power over humanity and earth, and, of course, about amassing maximum wealth. But a true seeker of Truth of his own will get help from the Lord in various ways, so that he can discover or find the Truth. The false projections out of the Darkness, however, again want to lead the seeker away from the Truth. Often Saint Jesus, Mary, or some angel appears and gives people meaningless or false information to simply mislead them.

THE MOST IMPORTANT THING FOR MAN IS TO KNOW THE ETERNAL LAWS OF GOD WELL, SO THAT HE CAN IMMEDIATELY DETERMINE WITH CERTAINTY WHETHER WHAT IS SAID OR SHOWN IS POSSIBLE AT ALL!

6. For every one of us who falls for the lies, believes them and spreads them further, this behaviour will have fatal consequences.

My own experience of the last years with Lucifer and his fallen angels was, and still is, how they try to hide the apparition of the Primordial Queen Elisabeth and Imanuel in 1917 in Fatima, by projections, which they show and spread everywhere on earth. Among so many wrong things, mankind did not recognize the real and true apparition. And humanity believed that it was the apparition of Mary and the little Saint Jesus just because the Church claimed it. Read the chapter on the Revelation of John, where it is explained thoroughly and truthfully (*Eternal Laws, Volume 1*).

Characteristic is the latest statement of mankind, which refers to messages from outer space (Pleiades) or uses other sources (about 10% real, 90% dark fallen angels) to assert that real hell does not exist at all. Consequently, for them there is only hell, which every human being builds up in his soul and therefore suffers from. This claim can be found in several videos or Internet sites. When someone leaves the church because he finds it untrustworthy, he falls straight into this more modern, esoteric trap.

And so the Darkness reached its goal. Almost everyone on earth is convinced that he will end up in heaven after his earthly death. These people probably forgot one of the Laws of God: "What you sow, you *must* reap many times."

EACH ONE OF US IS FULLY RESPONSIBLE FOR HIS BELIEFS AND HIS ACTIONS!

7. The difference between Spirit and Soul

Surely you wonder whether I was already a believer before my coma, or only afterwards. By "believer" I of course mean my faith in the Lord, and not in church teachings. As with love, man's faith in the Lord is a thing of his heart—of his spirit and nothing else. In the book *Grail Message*, as well as in the book *Eternal Laws*, I read that spirit and soul are something completely different, and mutually exclusive. There I had the opportunity to ask my teacher why millions of people make no distinction at all between spirit and soul. The answer was once again very simple:

"Come, I'll show you in a picture what a big, significant difference it is." Suddenly a very fine screen projection of the Spiritual Realm appeared before us. "What kind of fog is there, what is it anyway?" I asked him, and he replied:

"This is the most distant cloak of our Lord. From that we all come, which we are to mature in the World of Matter. In the Spiritual Realm the Lord created the spirit germs, which are then to incarnate on earth in bodies, where they need many earthly lives (200 to 500) for their own spiritual maturing. But the most important things are the abilities of the spirit, which are the only ones that enable him to connect with the Heights, so that he can present his petitions and thanks to the Lord. And another important thing: only the spirit can receive the living power from God."

Now everything else became clear to me. We feel the spirit close to our hearts through the warmth that God's power gives us to live. The ethereal cloak of the spirit is the soul; then comes another cloak, the earthly body. The cloaks are necessary so that the spirit can sink to earth through the Law of Gravity.

HE WHO TURNS AWAY FROM THE LORD HUMILIATES HIS SPIRIT BY ALLOWING HIMSELF TO BE GUIDED ONLY BY THE THOUGHTS OF HIS INTELLECT, AND CAN NO LONGER ABSORB THE POWER GIVEN TO HIM BY GOD.

8. The Truth of Reincarnation, and the Law of Gravity

Can you imagine how much effort and work it took the Darkness to cover up the Truth just to bring humanity into this miserable situation it finds itself in today?

- The murders of the prophets.
- The murder of Abdrushin, Son of Light, and of Saint Jesus.
- In the third century, the next servant of the Darkness appeared: the Emperor Constantine. The Church at that time was already so corrupt that it bribed the Emperor to burn the real Bibles, and afterwards only the Church's Bible version could be distributed among mankind. So it came about that the real Bibles have only become pocket books to this day.
- The Second Council of Constantinople (553 A.D.) also led to further deletions, in which the reincarnation according to the Law of God was completely removed from the Bible. The only goal was, again, to gain the greatest possible power over people and to amass wealth, because influence and wealth belong together.

Perhaps you will not believe me that the Roman Catholic Church claims to this day that we only have one life on earth. Because of this, each one of us has to buy freedom from our sins —quite a good trick, isn't it? But then how is it possible for one to live in wealth while another is homeless? Something is certainly not right here, and as always we recognize the lies of the churches, innumerable ranks of religious circles and other communities. My teacher explained everything to me briefly and clearly:

"The Darkness reached its goal again, because the people fell into the trap again. It wanted to make mankind on earth believe that the LORD is unjust. Never forget: God the Father is not just, He is the **purest Justice** in Himself and in His Eternal Laws! And His Eternal Laws continue to work incorruptibly and inviolably, regardless of whether mankind knows them or believes in the teachings of the Church. You know, the perfection of His Laws is shown by the fact that they do not allow exceptions. Those who believe in the Holy God and in the Truth will receive bliss and love as a harvest that will lead them back to their home as mature spirits in Creation. Now you can also imagine where the indifferent and the dark spirits must sink. Of course: into the depths, to hell, depending on how dense, dark, and heavy they made their spiritual cloak-soul throughout their lives, and all that without anyone forcing them to do it. On earth it's called sin."

I see. With their free will the people decided for themselves and thereby formed the heaviness of their cloak.

EVERYONE IS, IN REALITY, AT HOME WHERE THEY WERE CREATED BY GOD THE FATHER.

9. Other medieval lies became big traps

Everywhere you can see statues of Mary (sometimes also with a crown of 12 stars), as well as the infinite rows of wooden crosses. We already know that the Primordial Queen Elisabeth wears the 12 stars as her crown, with each star symbolising a creation. We learned that there are 12 more creations under the Primordial Creation. That's what I had to ask the teacher. I was glad he just got here.

I spoke to him: "Are there really 12 creations in the universe? And how is the Lord able to provide all with his power?"

"His power is infinite. After the battle against the Darkness/Lucifer, He can create another 12 if He so desires. But today we have completely different learning topics."

The Cult around Mary

"Humanity bows to every statue or representation that reminds us of Saint Jesus or Mary. But!!! It is only allowed to bow before the Lord in order to show Him respect. The Darkness has brought mankind to this nonsense through the churches. You bow (90%) to an item and you will stay there. It all began in medieval times with the assertion that Mary was the Primordial Queen, who thus received a greater worship than the Lord.

Saint JESUS and His Task

"At the same time, the Jesuits (a part of the Roman Catholic Church) also claimed that Saint Jesus appeared on earth only so that he could take upon himself the sins of mankind. And almost everyone believes this nonsense to this day. Too bad!"

Confession

"Confession was also invented during the Inquisition. Thus the Jesuits from Spain learned everything about the people who stood in their way (the royal couple Isabella of Castile and Ferdinand of Aragon). For the Jesuits wanted to have the whole world under their power. The confession helped them to discover so-called heretics and witches, and so they burned 14 million people as inquisitors of the Church—of course they were innocent! Confession cannot free anyone, for each one of us is responsible for all of his own sins. Confession and the remission of sins by the Church are all lies of the Church. Saint Jesus could not take all our sins upon himself according to the Eternal Laws! That's the Church's biggest lie! This gave rise to the legend that Saint Jesus only incarnated on earth so that he could free mankind from its sins, and then they live on happily ever after."

God's Law is, "What you sow, you **must** reap!"

FROM THE SONS OF GOD TO THE SMALLEST CREATURES, IN ALL 12 CREATIONS, NO ONE HAS THE ABILITY TO TAKE UPON HIMSELF THE SINS OF OTHERS. SUCH AN ABILITY DOES NOT EXIST AT ALL!

10. Hell

More appropriate would be the title: "What I was allowed to see from hell." Once again it was a projection on the already mentioned screen. Before that, I already noticed that the teachers steer the screen projection by their strong will, as well as many other things that we do not know on earth. In the beginning, I saw the dark planes from -1 to -7. Below, there was a big shape that resembled a gigantic funnel. (see fig. Structure of the Creation)

Luckily, my teacher sat next to me and explained everything to me.

I asked him, "What kind of planets are underground?"

"You call this part of the universe hell. Old planets, which already fulfilled their tasks and services, sink in free fall into the funnel in which they disintegrate, namely into the elementary particles from which they were created by God the Father. Of course, these elementary particles rise again behind the funnel, back to their owner."

"And what happens to the billions of spirits and beings that live on this planet?" I asked.

"First, I want to—or have to—explain to you how the will of God and its Eternal Laws value man, namely according to the heaviness of his ethereal cloaks. Only then is it possible for you to understand the answer to your question. God the Father only wants to take back into His Creation those spirits and beings who have decided out of free will to return to Him, thus want to live in their homeland and in eternity—in paradise. God the Father and Imanuel are only interested in the final radiation (currently the last one) and the maturity of each spirit or being. How many mistakes they had made in all previous earthly lives in order to reach this state of maturity is of no interest to Imanuel as judge at all. For Him, only the result is important. God the Father never wants to have those in Creation whose conviction is based on coercion. For the Lord, it is only worthwhile if spirits or beings voluntarily choose him. Your question is again about the soul of every spirit or being. So we must consider how heavy the ethereal cloaks of each of us became in the course of all our earthly lives. Those with bright, transparent souls are light and naturally ascend to their homeland. The dark and heavy cloaks sink into the caves, so deep, until they meet their kind in the depth. They may spend centuries there until they understand their sins against the Laws of God and want to change. In other words, until they can cast off their dark cloaks because they make amends for their sins."

If I hadn't really seen all this, I would find it hard to believe. As Imanuel, for example, describes the blind servants of churches in the book *Resonances to the Grail Message:* they cannot continue in the depth behind a magnetic wall consisting of poles, and must stay there until they acknowledge the truth and thus lay aside the cover of the ecclesial lies. Only then is it possible for them to get through between the poles.

But, in this land of twilight, there are many millions of detainees. They all apologize for what the churches taught them. They live in eternal darkness and cold, without nature. They're misguided, lost spirits. And I didn't see what lies even deeper. Even more lost, suffering from great pain in their souls, are those who committed suicide. They continuously experience their depressions around themselves and their suicide anew, until they realize again what a gift from God their life on earth was and what value it had—certainly not such a diminutive value as to have just thrown it away frivolously. They certainly remember the subject matter from their school days, according to which the earth is becoming increasingly dense. This is true, and only so could it happen that the earth sank from its natural place to the regions of Darkness (planes -2/-3). Only for this reason was it possible for the dark ones to incarnate on earth.

Imanuel, by his magnetic power, will pull the earth up again where it belongs and was created—as the last bright planet in Creation. Everything has been running for several years, so that the earth must leave all those (indifferent and dark spirits) who do not belong to it at all. I don't want to scare them, but that's the truth.

THE MORE LOVE AND HELP MAN GIVES OUT IN HIS LIFE, THE FASTER HE RETURNS TO HIS HOME.

11. The Excuses: Fate or Curse

One of the most common excuses is that of fate. There are thousands of excuses, if not more. However, there are only two possible decisions of will for each human being: yes or no. When someone comes home drunk, for example (and this applies to any addiction), an alcoholic says: "I had to drink with my friends because..." That's a lie! The worst thing about it is that such a person also lies to himself and believes his own lies. But the truth sounds like this: "I drank because I wanted to drink."

Another, for example, makes a promise but does not keep it. Again you hear the excuse: " I couldn't do it because..." I'm sure you can guess what the truth sounds like: "I didn't do it because I didn't want to do it."

My teacher came. He knew exactly what I was thinking about. So I asked him right away:

"What will happen to these people if their whole life on earth consists of such lies?"

"That's either self-deception or dreaming, because man is running away from the truth. But it keeps catching up with him. In addition, he constantly suffers from stress and anxiety. Of course, his spiritual cloaks are getting heavier and denser, with every lie aggravating this. Spiritually he sinks deeper and deeper, towards the lowest point of hell. It's a failed life. Do not forget: the Divine Power is always in motion, it can never stop. It either moves upwards according to its lightness, or it must sink downwards in a condensed form. After a few generations, people are content with the fact that it is their fate or that there is a curse on the whole family. In truth, it shows either their mental sluggishness, or their conscious suppression of the truth. In the end, such a person has dense, dark soul cloaks after many earthly lives. Such a one then ponders with his mind, but never comes to a solution, for his spiritual intuitive perception remain excluded."

WITHOUT INTUITIVE PERCEPTION SUCH A PERSON REMAINS COLD, RUTHLESS AND ALL FRIENDS AND ACQUAINTANCES LEAVE HIM. ALL HIS EARTHLY LIVES HE MUST SPEND IN SOLITUDE.

12. Where are IMANUEL'S heralds?

Surely you remember the old prophets who proclaimed the Messiah, Jesus. By the way, He was not recognized as such by mankind anyway. The older Son of God, Imanuel, had and has many more helpers whose task it was—and still is—to proclaim openly and truly on earth that He will be the future Saviour of the World of Matter.

Let me start all over again. Before the coming of Abdrushin (1,000 B.C.), forerunners lived on earth: from Hjalfdar to Lao-Tse, Zoroaster, Krishna and Mohammed, who were to spread the Truth in all corners of the earth that the Son of God is Imanuel, the Will of God. Their successors, however, twisted their teachings and built up their own cults and religious doctrines.

The heralds who followed these forerunners were either murdered, misjudged, or distracted by the Darkness. One of the distracted was Rudolf Steiner, who exaggerated himself and even developed his own philosophy (anthroposophy) instead of proclaiming the Son of God Imanuel.

Swanhild was the only one who truly proclaimed Him as "the Truth and Justice". (*Eternal Laws, Volume 3*)

Imanuel prophesied: "All over the earth, thousands will rise and announce me."

But as always, there was a lack of devotion to service, and there was great disappointment, to which we all contributed through our fear or disinterest.

13. I'm sure you won't like these truths

Once upon a time there was Planet Earth, whose inhabitants caused its ever-deeper fall. It was and is strategically the most important planet, as the deepest in Creation. Why this? Very simple: God the Father sends the neutral principal power into the vessel of the Holy Grail. As soon as the White Dove—Imanuel—appears above it, this power sinks through the whole of Creation to the last planet, that is to say to the earth, so that people can receive and process it. Processed, the power then rises again, back to her owner. But!!! The owner gets back only 3% of the processed power. The remaining 97% is also processed by mankind, but negatively and thus condensed, so that they voluntarily give it to the Darkness instead of to the Light, mostly ignorantly. By this disturbance of the natural circuit of the principal power, the earth sank from light planes of Creation to low dark planes (planes between -2 and -3; see fig. Structure of the Creation).

How did it get this far? Lucifer came down with a third of the angels to teach humanity how to use its earthly intellect, thus helping it to find its way back to the light more quickly. At first he saw himself as the steward of all materiality. After a short time, however, he became so arrogant that he called himself the ruler of the Word of Matter. From then on, the angels, who had fallen with Lucifer, instilled into people's minds only negative thoughts (avarice, envy, rage). And again, it was mankind that followed these whispers, and thus let the evil arise. If there was no human who could be seduced, the Last Judgement would have been greeted joyfully, and would not have had to take on the forms that we experience every day, even if many do not want to see or accept it.

Of course, together with everything else, the **femininity** also fell. God the Father created the woman in such a way that she can see higher into the Creation and thus stands spiritually elevated. In this way she can describe to the man what she has seen with her finer intuitive perception and guide him. The man then puts this into action. Therefore, men were created by God the Father physically bigger and stronger than the women. It is a great lie to claim that women are only on earth to have children. Their true values show primarily in their intuitive perception. Maternity comes second.

If we take all this together, we come to only one conclusion: we are in the middle of the Last Judgment, and have been for a few years. Hence there is also the Star of the Son of Man in the sky, also called Great Comet.

There's only one way we can get out of this mess: he who decides, of his own free will to become again an inwardly light person gets **the chance in the Kingdom of the Millennium to further develop himself and thus to save himself from disintegration. Today there is still the possibility to choose, but in a few weeks there will be no more time to do so.**

THERE'S NO MORE TIME TO HESITATE, BELIEVE IT OR NOT.

14. Purgatory

It wasn't long ago that I was told to write the truth about what this term actually means. It is clear that the churches give many words a completely different meaning than they mean in reality.

Purgatory refers to a place where the bright ones lay down their astral cloak (body, mantle). It is that simple. On earth we lay down our gross-materiality cloak and then it is the astral, fine ethereal cloak turn. So everyone must gradually remove all the different cloaks of the spirit until they enter the Spiritual Realm. But this applies only to the bright spirits who have completed their necessary maturing process in the World of Matter and hurry back to their real homeland so that they can reach eternal life there.

It is one of the greatest lies of the churches that, according to them, everyone, whether a sinner or not, washes himself completely clean of his sins in purgatory and then ascends to heaven. A man who has voluntarily accepted dark covers must not approach purgatory at all. Why? Thanks to his dark covers he became too heavy and his own, voluntarily chosen heaviness pulls him down to hell.

WHAT WE OURSELVES THINK ABOUT OURSELVES CAN ULTIMATELY BE THE OPPOSITE OF WHAT THE LORD SEES IN US.

15. The Prayer

Until my coma I did not know exactly whether my prayers and gratitude were in order according to the Eternal Laws. So my first question to the oldest one was:

"Please, explain to me which prayer is the real, true one and which is the wrong one. And why it's wrong."

"For you everything has to be logically understandable and thorough, right? You have known for several years that only your mind has the necessary ability to connect to the Source. Only God the Father is the Source of everything." He looked at me and knew I hadn't understood anything yet.

"The prayer goes the same way as all other energies of God the Father, because He is the only Source. If you on earth call this energy 'prayer', that does not change the Laws of the Lord at all. Only your spirit can connect so high that your prayers come to Him. And all the others are wrong because they do not have the strength to ascend to God the Father.

To help you understand this: The prayers learned by heart only with the mind are completely powerless, since they do not come from the spirit (pure heart). Like a bad recitation of a poem. They just fall apart on earth, in the astral."

"I know people who pray several times a day and know hundreds of lines." I replied.

"They should live their short time on earth much more purposefully. But they made their choice, so it's their problem.

"And now to the earthly texts of the prayers: all these have been invented by the church authorities. The true prayers are those which God's Sons left to mankind. And, of course, also those which man says to the Lord with his own words from the heart (gratitude, request for help and other things)".

That was a really good explanation and it all became clear to me. The intuitive perception of the spirit are energetically the strongest in a human being. Therefore, only they are able to ascend to the height of the Source. In other words: prayers full of love and devotion become powerful radiations and automatically rise to God the Father according to the Law of Gravity.

"Look here," my teacher said. On the screen I saw golden and silver stars rising higher and higher.

My teacher continued, "All these are prayers that ascend to the Lord. The golden ones come from adults who are bright and mature. The silver ones come from the spirits of pure children."

"May I see what it looks like around the world?"

"Yes, but there is rarely anything beautiful to see."

The teacher was right: from the radiation of the dark ones I saw only a black mass and here and there golden or silver stars of the bright ones were to be seen. It immediately became clear to me that the earth can only be saved by the Holy Spirit, Imanuel, because mankind is too weak to do so. The Will of God is Truth and Justice.

IMANUEL IS OUR REAL HOPE AND SALVATION!

16. How to live? Self-destructive or self-healing?

My sympathetic teacher is already sitting on the grass. Why?

"Come on, girl. I have already indicated to you that today's conversation will only be understood by those who really want it. And of the new friends, only those who want to learn it out of their own free will. First, I want to say that earthly medicine has disappointed me very much."

"Why's that?" I asked.

"When the first pills were made, people welcomed them more and more. In the end, however, they were only concerned that they no longer had to work on themselves with their own strong free will in this way. They rely more on the effect of the pills than they believe in themselves. This is completely incomprehensible to me.

"And now comes the serious part of the lesson: my memory tells me that the teacher and the doctor should not work separately from each other, but in one person—that is how humanity has changed.

"A good teacher explains everything precisely, but also in a simple way. You surely know that all diseases come from problems of the soul, because the cause of the disease is in the soul. Man is supposed to put this cause in order, and therefore heal it, and not fight the consequences in and on the body. The earthly body is treated on earth for decades—often until death, but the healing of the cause goes fast and as a result the physical illness is soon over.

"If, for example, a person is negative and pessimistic in his life, he or she has often abandoned the right path to the LORD for many years and is far away from it. Now the earthman think, 'What's wrong with it? Almost every human behaves in the same way on earth.' That excuse is wrong and totally cowardly.

"You know, girl. Anyone who lives so pessimistically is hard and uncomfortable with others, and also commits suicide in his subconscious. Whether people know about it or not, nothing changes and the result is always the same.

"Man thinks that all this belongs to the light sins only. But, he sucks the life energy out of his family, relatives, and colleagues and doesn't even know it.

"The more serious the sin, the deeper he sinks down to the dark planes of hell. And all those who, even deliberately, out of free will, commit these sins, can no longer free themselves from them because the time necessary for this is getting shorter and shorter. And so they sink to where they belong."

"Please, let me take a deep breath and work on today's topic. Could we continue tomorrow? Please, please," I asked.

"Of course, get some rest."

I stayed behind with my mouth open; my teacher stood up, went away and taught others.

17. From the first day of man to life in the Millennium

At school, I could never believe that humans originated from monkeys. Something else had to have happened. The teacher came and I smiled.

"Yes. I know you're curious about everything you don't understand from top to bottom. Today will be interesting. Where should I start?"

"To earth came first with nature the elemental beings, then the animals. Today it is taught that from the animals (monkeys) mankind has developed. This can't be true!"

"You're right. What mankind does not know, it fills these gaps with its own ideas and so all the legends arose which mankind believes today. In the beginning, the elemental beings who preserve nature to this day came to earth with nature. Then thousands of years passed until the Lord saw (in the first civilization of the earth, Lemuria) that the monkeys (manganese) were physically developed enough to allow the first spirits to incarnate into them. This is what happened then. But most of the elemental beings had to return to their homeland (e.g. the giants who built the pyramids), because mankind, with their short-term stays on earth, destroyed all possibilities of living together with them."

"What? And why?"

"The dark ones could never get enough gold, money and wealth. So they came to the conclusion that they could make money out of the forests themselves. Many animal species became extinct as a result and their keepers—the elemental beings—left the earth. So did the giants. And you can see for yourself how humanity developed through the exercise of its free will."

"And what happened next?"

"Thousands of years passed again, and the Lord saw that mankind needed much help."

"May I ask you a question?" The teacher nodded in response.

"I've heard many versions, but what is the truth about the Millennium?"

"Technically very easy and logically explained: the earth is overcrowded with dark people. The first to leave the earth, in the event of natural disasters, are the indifferent. Then the bright ones and the earth itself will be saved by Imanuel. Ultimately, Imanuel will pull the Earth up by his magnetic power, about half the distance from Creation. It can't get any higher because all the poisons have made it so heavy. And according to the Law of Gravity, the earth must not rise higher. But through the same Law of God all the dark ones also fall away from her and must sink down to their kind. In the meantime, the elemental beings are rebuilding Mount Zion and purifying the earth of its poisonous cloak."

"And when will all this come?"

"No one knows the exact date, only the Lord knows it. But one thing is for sure: it will happen in your present life."

NEVER FORGET: THE PEAK OF PURIFICATION BEGINS WITH NATURAL DISASTERS.

18. The Millennium

The mysterious Kingdom of the Millennium never went out of my mind. Everybody said something different about it, but it just didn't make sense.

"Yeah, yeah, girl. The churches and sects turn the help of the Lord into meaningless speeches. Too bad." Only now I've noticed that my teacher is sitting next to me.

"And what's the truth?" I asked.

"Above all, always tell people the truth. When the time comes, they'll remember everything. The purpose of the Millennium is to save the bright people and the earth itself. The bright ones will await the transition period sheltered in a very beautiful place."

"And how long will that take?"

"It will be very brief. Just until the elemental beings have repaired everything that liquidated mankind. Don't worry, the elemental beings are very proficient and very quick. After a few weeks, the bright ones will return to the repaired earth."

"Do you know what the churches and sects tell people?" I asked.

"Mankind on earth lives spiritually in lies. And the worst thing about it is that man also lies to himself and believes it." But now back to our subject. Mount Zion will be rebuilt on earth, the bright ones will adorn Jerusalem to receive their King, Imanuel, full of dignity, honour and love."

"So, everything happens on Earth? No paradise and no permanent place before the throne of God?" I asked.

"All lies to make a few feel powerful and superhuman when they promise people all sorts of things."

THE CHURCH TELLS FAIRY TALES TO MANKIND. THIS IS ONE OF ITS GREATEST SINS. WE DON'T HAVE TO BELIEVE THESE FAIRY TALES.

19. Apocalypse and "The Last Day"

As always, or rather, uninterruptedly, I sat in the meadow and thought about the difference between these two terms, when they are supposed to mean the same thing.

"Well, you girl, it's all wrong," my teacher said.

"What is wrong with it if we imagine it on earth in such a way that one word, as well as the other, is to designate the end of mankind and many planets. Or is it all a lie again?" I asked.

"First, the ignorance of the translators who contributed to the misinterpretation becomes clear. Apocalypse means that all truths kept secret come to light at God's command. And that's what's happening now. The apocalypse of individual people, peoples or present states means that their honour and power are to be destroyed because all their false moves are uncovered. The present apocalypse concerns the churches and their lies."

"You say present, but when will the last day come for Earth?"

"After the salvation of all the bright ones by Imanuel comes the time of the Kingdom of the Millennium. When the bright people in the Kingdom become able to live according to the Laws of God, they are allowed to return to their spiritual homeland."

"And when will the end of the earth come?"

Again he laughed at my question: "Never!!! The Lord decided that the earth, no matter where it is, remains the last planet of Creation forever. Exactly for this reason it will rise in a thousand years to become the Spiritual Realm. Then the Spiritual and the Primordial Spiritual will already form a Realm.

The last event will be that everything under the Spiritual Realm sinks into disintegration. Hell, with the people who did not want to live according to the Will of God, then the whole World of Matter and also the Ring of the animistic beings. For the Lord created them only for the spirits, that they might mature spiritually in materiality."

Imanuel and Swanhild described this very precisely. According to Imanuel, this event will last 1500 years. But as always, humanity misunderstood it and it was exploited by the Darkness. Everything I read about IMANUEL and Swanhild suddenly became clear to me. Yes, as the earth will rise, in every Realm it must lay down its crusts and cloaks.

One word and how many mistakes!

AS OUR LORD SAID: WE SHOULD CONSIDER EVERY WORD CAREFULLY UNTIL WE PRONOUNCE IT OUT LOUD!

20. Farewell

All three oldest ones, my teachers, came to me. This is going to be interesting today, I thought.

"Yes, very interesting. This time it's about you."

I forgot to breathe and looked at the screen. I saw something there that looked like a night sky.

"It's not a night. This is the astral cloak of the earth. There hasn't been a 'blue planet' for over 100 years. Now remember exactly what it looks like."

"And what do the stars and the flames mean? They will be wiped out shortly?"

"Well, yeah. These are the people who are waiting for you because they need help."

The third teacher said, "But you can choose: You may stay here, or go back into your body and continue your earthly life to help. You may get some abilities from our Lord, but your earthly life will be very painful for your body. And you will also need a lot of patience."

"How long have I been here?"

"According to earth time, eight months and three days today."

"And what happened to my physical (earthly) body during that time? Is it still usable?"

"Yes, your body is in a coma in an army hospital in Switzerland. An earthly, elderly doctor, the best friend of your late husband, is looking after it."

"I have one last question. Where are my husband and son?"

"At home, among the highest angels. They love you very much and are waiting for you. As your last task you will help people and heal them, either physically or psychologically. However, this will take several years. For this reason, God the Father gives you supernatural abilities and a lot of patience. Those before you forgot their duties. You will have to replace them, in addition to your task (fulfil their task.)"

After these last words I found myself back in the tunnel and saw how some were waving to me and wishing me success.

2nd Part

THE ETERNAL LAWS
As they were explained to me

The Laws of God have already been explained to mankind four times:

- 3000 years ago by Abdrushin
- 2000 years ago by Jesus
- 90 years ago by Imanuel
- 20 years ago by Swanhild

Of course I don't belong to the Sons of God or Swanhild. The Laws of God were explained to me in my coma by the oldest ones. If I look around, I currently see 2 to 3% bright people. So I decided to write the Laws of God down and make them more understandable for the 3% by explaining their meanings:

1. **The Law of Reciprocal Action** (called the law of karma by many) provides justice in truth. You probably already know what it is about: helping others or the sins of individuals. This is what you can learn from it: what we radiate or give today, this Law brings us back several times.
   We alone are building our future.

2. **The Law of Attraction of Homogeneous Species** provides harmony. Sure, I have already mentioned that all energies are magnetic and that every single species has its never-changing colour.
   Depending on how we radiate, we attract people like that.

3. **The Law of Completing a Unit**. This is not about attracting the same species, but about divisions of species that want to reunite to form a species. This Law makes this possible. Otherwise no one could find his complement.

4. **The Law of Gravity** provides order in all creations. It basically means that a dark one can never come up or vice versa, a bright one cannot fall into hell.
How heavy our spiritual cloaks are is up to us.

5. **The Law of Motion** does not only provide for body movement to maintain health. It is also about the energies in the body, mainly the energies around us. How unpleasant and tired we must often feel when surrounded by negative colleagues or relatives. In short, they suck our energy away. This happens, for example, when you radiate just a little bit of fear. No one can hurt you unless you let them. Fear is one of these possibilities. So look up to the LORD, raise your head and realize your goals joyfully.
If one does not pursue a spiritual goal, one's life on earth is meaningless.

6. **The Law of Equilibrium** is simple. In the beginning we take our life from the LORD, and then daily His daylight and His warmth. If we are grateful to Him, we have nothing to be afraid of. And in life? Only to the extent that we give our feelings, patience and love to others do we acquire the right to claim these gifts.
Who always only gives selflessly, their radiation will be bright and beautiful. Who only demands and takes, reaches the black darkness.

7. **The Law of the Development** can be experienced consciously or unconsciously. If we live according to the Laws of God, this Law ensures eternal ascent into and within Creation. In our spirit everything becomes clearer and more loving little by little. Only then can we remember in our spiritual memory everything that happened in all our previous lives.

Whoever lives against the Laws of God can never be happy but will only live depressed in solitude. If we could combine all the colours of these Laws of God (energies), we would get the purest white light. On earth this is the energy of healing. All Laws of God lead to the Love of God. For us, it means our own selfless devotion.

Abdrushin, Autor of the Book
In the Light of Truth, Grail Message, 1931 (IMANUEL)

IMANUEL, the Real Saviour of the Earth

Natalia de Lemeny Makedonova, autor of the Book
Eternal Laws, Volume 1 -3, 1997 – 1998 (SWANHILD)

SWANHILD

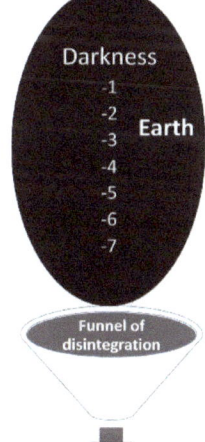

GOD
Unsubstantiate Realm
Jesus   Imanuel
(Son of God)   (Holy Spirit)

Elisabeth
(Primordial Queen, Divine Mother)

Divine Realm

Primordial Spiritual
Realm

Spiritual Realm
Mary
(Earthly mother of Jesus)

Animistic Realm

Ethereal World
Gross Material World

Darkness
-1
-2
-3   Earth
-4
-5
-6
-7

Funnel of
disintegration

Fundamental particles

FSC
www.fsc.org
MIX
Papier | Fördert
gute Waldnutzung
FSC® C083411

Zeitfracht Medien GmbH
Ferdinand-Jühlke-Straße 7
99095 Erfurt, Deutschland
produktsicherheit@kolibri360.de